Strands

Patrick WILLI

GW00600644

PALORES PUBLICATIONS' 21st CENTURY WRITERS

Patrick Williamson
Strands

July 2008

ISBN 978-0-9556682-9-6

Published by:

Palores Publications,
11a Penryn Street,
Redruth,
Cornwall.
TR15 2SP

Designed and printed by:

ImageSet,
63 Tehidy Road,
Camborne,
Cornwall.
TR14 8LJ
01209 712864

Typeset in:
Times New Roman 11/12pt
Tahoma 14/14

Other publications

Poetry:
- *In memory of my grandfather*, Libanus Press, 1986.
- *Lobster eating* 1997; *Selection FIP: The English Equivalent* 2003, all Macan Press.
- *Quarante et un poètes de la Grande-Bretagne*, (ed.) Ecrits des Forges/ Les Temps des Cerises, 2003
- *Amsterdam, Rougement (artists' books)*, Transignum and Pli, *2004 and 2005*
- *Poezia* (selected poems, in Bulgarian), Nov Zlatorog, 2006
- *Prussia Cove*, Palores Publications, 2007

Translations:
- *The films of Jacques Tati*, (co-trans.) Guernica, Toronto 1997.
- *Ocean Routes*, En Vues, 1998.
- Tahar Bekri, *Inconnues Saisons/Unknown Seasons* (selected poems, co-trans), Ed. L'Harmattan, 1999.
- Gilles Cyr, *Graph of Roads* (selected poems, co-trans), Guernica Editions, 2008
- Serge Pey, *Every poem is a decapitated head held up by a single hair* (poems, co-trans; with Yann Lovelock), publisher pending

Acknowledgements
Some of these poems or versions of these poems, have appeared in the following magazines in the UK, Europe and North America:

Combats, Decanto, Envoi, First Time, Heidelberg Review, Nth position, Ore, Pennine Platform, Upstairs in Duroc.

Surety and *Commandment* are found poems based on Proverbs 6.

Coverart: *Great Blaster from the West* by Norman Ackroyd, reproduced with kind permission of the artist.

Acknowledgment for back cover quotes: Alain Corbin, *The Lure of the Sea. The discovery of the seaside 1750-1840*, translated by Joselyn Phelps (London: Penguin Books, 1994), James Midgeley in a review for Sphinx/ Happenstance.

Contents

Arrival

Weaving burgundy-grey crowds -
a streaming wartime orphan
clutching a leather case with labels
to Brighton, Vienna, Budapest,
the Cornish Riviera... shunts

along the shore, inlet after inlet, as
a coaster halts at dead of night,
and barrels plunge in, marke the spot
as seas swirl the fo'castle slip
away down smoothed rails

standard bearing through breach
of sea, a blaze in dazzling
golden heat, the prow strikes so

stumble into the undertow
foam specked skin
dark as mahogany, dripping
a tropic night, screech

we hit the buffers
expelled air hisses
step down into grey
Penzance.

Atrium

The wind has gone, the stained light fragments:
I survey undulating masses, cross the atrium,
take note of all possible intrigues, there
the curtained window turns light & time
soot-black, here my apostolic companions
talk in feverish languages, moist respiration
born-again faces, whorls printed in ash, with avid
hands raised, I grip the creed as Stentor cries,
they prostrate before the unconquered sun.

Then, at Alban Arthuan, the star stood over:
with oblivious hope welling in the darkness, she
crushed grain in her shadowy hold, lit the fire
in the lee of the wattled wall, saying - emerge
from the night of enclosure into blinding nature.

Movement

The rains are chasing me
past the Witan-stone of Morwenstow,
grey black clouds folding
silver cloth.

Blonds reeds grow from the nimble earth
the waterlogged earth,
pearls embedded in the wind's hands.

Pale blue washed out clouds
hiding the fire
move gently on
unstoppable, unshakeable.

Watch, they skilfully tack
across the oceans of the sky.

Cudden point

We walk along the tumbling cliffs,
along the path of Hosts, multitudes singing
above the squalls, & the sheer
tumult below charges forward,
reaching up, sliding back, one step
forward, reach out & slip back.

The lee winds up to the dragon's eye,
wind whispers by our feet & lichen creeps
& the sun flexes its dying strength, reflecting
water into bitter fragments; let's bury
the hatchet, Brigitte, make up and just be
so the flock sleeps by night, and Love

on our side of the earth, a rockbound shelter
we talk of candlewax and harlequins,
& sometimes of little, sometimes not at all,
we barely see the seams of existence.

Leave

In the garden of Auntie May,
and Uncle Jack, there is the strangeness,
the oak hall chest, my trunk,
the rushing silk of stocking'd feet,
perfume of market stalls, the heat,
mystery.

The clerk's walrus moustache barks gruffly,
his pungent pipe smoke signals
the fire that
oils our pistons and
now propels us forward,
sinew stretches, flows
unrestrained harmonies
as if never before known
these silences & songs,
songs of wise men's tales,
raging seas, rolling iron
vats of steam, broken spells
and Fagins that beckon
& sneer, saying, " Come, boy,
come play for me. Steal,
& there'll always be something to eat. "

Isserlis

His deep tones reap the vivid roll call
pictures posed behind
the glass he pauses to breathe
black tousled hair thrown back
alert face abruptly looking at the ceiling
as if in a trance, concentration
taut in his jaw he listens
to the rich seam, flitting fingers
almost disassociated
holding audiences in a church stillness

Drift

Boats condemned cut through thwarts
keels into four pieces, grip the rails
as the wash tumbles round the rock,
wintering all boats cheap rates:

we lower skyscrapers, scrap yard,
drift under the coast, make for Snyde,
night pools pit and pock all roads
so tighten our belt and lighten the scales,
hear me now - do not turn aside, do not

close your eyes to my voice
no man here shall be lost - it's close
the rustling reaches our prow, cast
out all the oil-skin bags, fearing
ballast, masts, bulk-heads taken out,
decks ripped fore and aft, we become

shards swept away, towed under
by the score, we committed
our fortunes to command, to Clauda
where two eyes meet, to run aground
beams asunder, bottom planks ripped off

hulls broken by waves, sawn
into four parts athwartships so
head and heart stuck fast
at the foot of the rock

Inland

Out walking, there are always subjects inland:
the time to reap, the rock detritus of a field.
Peter says it could be used as foundation -
one chooses stone by the quality of its grain.

Up from terrace to roof timbers, past the stage
of facade, we look through the church walls.

He once gathered skulls & bones from the yard,
piling the latter into neat heaps, building
a shelf to line the hollow-eyed up against a wall.
They stare straight through you, he said
he has snapshots to record the end of the work.

Move on, this is a complex mingling of our dust
steps taken towards it; relatives, then us
face to face with bullocks, nostrils quivering.

Blackberry fields

Inside, on the radio,
I hear all these worlds talking to me;
the weather they say, is overcast.

Outside by a birch, in blackberry
fields, in the whistling night.
I wait, but do not understand.

There are some empty baskets,
others, full of riches, creak.
The silence is divided by figures.

Here, among the brambles, bulbous
and purple with bitter juices,
selected in these final minutes.

I can see the thunder coming
and we still haven't finished
counting the fruit we have caught.

On the bare mountain side, I wander
through cloud to dazzling sea,
the landscape of centuries to come.

I find thorns that prick my skin,
blood flows unchecked,
the savagery knows no bounds.

Returning, with shards picked up
from the earth we trample,
sourness blackens our tongues.

Surety

if stricken with the hand of a stranger
you are

snared with the words
do this now my son and deliver yourself
make sure your friend
do not give sleep to your eyes
slumber to your eyelids
deliver yourself
as bird from the hand of the fowler
go to the ant, you sluggard
consider her ways, and be wise

yet a little sleep
a little slumber
a little folding of the hands to sleep

he winks with his eyes
speaks with his feet
teaches with his fingers
devises mischief continually
sows discord
suddenly he will be broken
without remedy

The prow of our voyage

Ice crusher of faith
& determination, single minded
pursuer of breath & winter light,
powering a course
through the known vision.

Strength breaks the ice-bound
rivers we skate on & cross,
where fishermen live
perched above their carved
rotund windows, open to the sea.

Depths of deep marine, my brother,
you now seem to contemplate
the white ice, the seams
of a forested foreshore, wind
scurried & rocky when breached.

We pick our way through untidy slabs,
walking on darkened waters
covered only by thick bottle-glass,
hard, lucid, incised
by the embedded cuts of old fractures.

Strands

Blinking blinking
down the line.
All ships to berth. Fog.

I

Strand-dwellers, we bustle,
among the strata of study,
engagement we thirst for
hidden as sun rips water

shreds our words
among the sucking molluscs
of the sea shore -

crunching the seashell mosaic
in the ebbing tide

we sort in the gusts
and lie caught by
                whether
life is ripe
or is it time

everything else
where the border runs
                nothing else
but us
                surf

II

Smoke with raging sailors
in a candlelit tavern, balcony ablaze

punctuated with shouts
rapier thrusts, a gage,

you flounder, shadow-walking waves
stranded, you are

in the firebrand throes of youth
the song remains the same;
young man of the eighties

this is where ideas first
stammered into being
long before I began
spluttering into life

III

Embark on
another strong brew, Ensor,
rest awhile, more have entered,
rest awhile on the bridge
endless conversing quests
while others fight
    justice
can be so

order, gentlemen, order,
notes are punctured holes
for the blind, from the first footfall

in the iron bound hulk, discover
what transcends is carnal,
by which I mean mortal issuance

they smoke stash
wander through ribs,
wrong-footed by wit,
flash, pulped in a gullet

IV

The first single blast, then
light-waves of memory
rolling in from the fog

the gates of the east, be honest
the flaking of each rock
changes little
           inside the inner circle
           pebbles shifted

stoke the dead man's rage
tentacle face

           (down the shore with you!)
storm
lash the face, cleanse us
     rage
fuel of reason
     know
freedom in clink
           do not go, do not go

in the dying of the light
age, world with one end
slug, gush, micturate

V

Ocean stirs up trouble,
the gusty sea of mist breaks,
lust grabs at pallid skin,
a passing spasm

lost somewhere in lashing rain,
he sprinkled grit, squeezed a sponge
against my forehead
    against the devil
that sent the cat into hiding
one night I entered a dive
near the ford,
    at the back
He stood with outstretched hands
whitewashed walls that harbour
the spirits, the welcome
of a wherryman
    today you are consigned, ashes
    strewn by the tide
open the depths, entrust yourself

VI

His skeletal hand, an imprint
on the window

                voices
that cascade into melt-waters,
the thread of allsouls

closer   much closer
closer to the ripples of your mouth

an immense sea-strength retains me
this is the treasure, the liberation
from the silt - the numen
essence uplifts,

this speech, these words
washing in the breeze

a gift.

Commandment

these seven things:
a proud look
a lying tongue
hands that shed innocent blood
a heart that devises wicked imagination
feet swift in running to mischief
a false witness that speaks lies
he who sows discord among brethren

bind them continually on your heart
and tie them around your neck

where you go it shall lead you
where you sleep keep you
when you awake talk to you

for it is a lamp
and the law is light
and reproofs are the way of life
to keep you
from the flattery of the tongue

The clumsy fisherman

for Kama Kamanda

Fish spill from his hands
as he stumbles through the water,
the sand, swirling
the world of passers-by, the clouds,
images of himself.

From his great height he ought to
spear them but instead
holds each wrestler in a handshake
of friendship, as they slip out,
rubbing their scales.

Birds flit around his head,
his mouth booming out greetings
the speed of an anchor chain
being pulled up from the depths,
rattling with good humour.

Way up in the sky, he sees
dark oceans driven
by the wind, &
sheep which have vertigo.

The sky overflows with dawns,
faces in the waters,
this night, this transparence
disappears & he sees
what exists & what no longer exists

there is no earth, time
has no importance,
the world is upside down
but the fisherman is everywhere,
gathering souls.

After the bal

A shoal of silver fish, swirling
under the street lamp
sparklers, strands of hair rushing
out of nowhere

thrust under artificial light
settling on a ice-sprinkled
bone handle knife of a road

that swathes night, walk
two by two into storm
flakes a sentence from the cold

scrape the windscreen, start up
Sunday dancing in sea light
down deserted slip roads

Harbour

Cruising up the silent ramparts
that harbour chattering
groups of teens illicitly smoking
on terraces that drop down to the sea
their back to the crashing
rush suck drive against the pulse
of ecstasy - eyes wide open, rigid

her boiling blood sluiced
through her membranes, fun-loving
not a drug addict - the sea knows them all
has engulfed thousands of them
you know who I mean -
rock broken and borne away yet
the night blinds them

as the tide retreats around the fort
the waves break to no audience
except the squeals of bravado
the ramparts hear in their stone hearts

Beach

Flathead mullet sweep into gullies
and waves crash over shrieking children
only the diving stone surfaces
out of the foam, shelf step into the dark
as we flip and flop on the sand
this mass of tanned/white marked flesh
we try to bury in remnants of stone
the dust of the bones of the earth

These turrets we built around
a floor-boarded silence
crack and drop into the sea
rock eroded by wind spume salt
tumbles onto rock

onto the land where the grumblies grow

Shore

in the freezing
in the freezing waters
buoyed by come and go, the
cries become distant and
body light
wash-away, wash-away the weight
of all I know
tousled hair becomes
a little cork barrier
encircling the breaking and
undertow that fills the bucket
in the freezing deep

it's the cold I write about
that feels warm once you're in
only when the wind chill sets in
sometime after, does the sun go cold
it's the water's silence that
not even the fish
not even the fish know
and whales
the dead forget the

Turnpike

Figures from a varnished oil
fissured by hearth-flames puff
from clay pipes that stretch forth
as pilgrim cocks his head

landlord hold court
ruminate the hours from night
intake between each
blessed are they
who speak to those that wait

in dark, as candle flickers
under rustling bush
on the highwayman's path
Old Tom, Jack, John Wiley
ale black inside pewter skull

far below sifting sands
may stone and light delve
into your core, may iron
gird your barrel, sink

tankards of rough but
do not judge the wood
strewn with tracks
we have to choose
respect what churns within.

Unbound

With apologies to Shelley

under the curdling winds an island
the peak on which we stand, midway
from the cliff, as whirlpools appeal

to the deep, to the deep
      down, down!
stillness there
and shades of sleep

no chains on these rocks, only the lonely
that drink and call truth an hour
of your hand upon me, and genius
a note that finds its string, blinded
    and justice
doubt, hurt, aggression
the shadow of some spirit lovelier still
to set free from the strait waistjacket
though evil stain and it shall be
a split hairpin, so fine
fall, both actor and victim
        down, down!
through the veil and the bar
things which seem and are
pummelled out by noise, haste
lest the world departs
    through the grey
the mists, wash me down
until, with one last look,
    I turn back

Flashback

We stand around the boiling heat,
like striplight flies attracted by the noise
of whispering through coupled hands,
and giants straddle the domed, smoking roof,
with their lagged lead pipes. We are bewitched

lovers exploring under the acacia trees of the heart,
in the Mistral, her mother's breath,
naked in the rocky river of goose pimples.

And at my cousin's close to Joyeux,
a feast, and in the moon-filled room, candlelit
crushed terra walls, companions
listening to Kodaly's voice - listen
to the uplift of cicadas in darkness.

Pale pear green, metà, chiavate,
Hale, dusty, lean, a cose fatte

Full of skinseams of flitting wonder
or moulds of others' withering trees,
your newly dug well brimming
drew in swirling patterns that merge:
before the sluice gate intervened,
an inlaid edge of life, lip and eye triggered
but not endeavour, flitting among your eaves.

These tendril hands

I pluck away, slight, metal fork pinned to the floor,
a skeleton to hold the score - my metronome body ticks.
Long crumpled hours feed as if I were mere liver.
cry bird and hollow stave, my rage, unjust as it might seem.
fingers tethered to rocks lashed by the Furies.

These tendril hands are throbbing pulses,
entangled weed knots cast onto the water.
I try to keep my stance in a certain balance,
firmly holding tongue until I lash a cheek.

Ace

Ace, search for action
shouldering cloth in post-toil glow
pluck from unseeing crowds
those approaching the bar
where Moose and Jas
are gambling, cast
a glance at these cards, get sharp,
standstill means you do not exist
in the stream of passage,
each random look, quick,
in thee I trust
make haste, upstairs
lowlit
    late night jazz
swims under smoky rafters
where plate glass reflects
spotlight and sunnight

Sue on keys, Lowri a mezzo
soaring above the murmurs,
we crouch, intently reliving
when the mango did the tango
down in Saint Tropez

Wake

Kisses punctuate
our movements
circumvent the centre space,
entrants turn
and bow their heads

leaving salt traces as they look,
the fibre of life
as his structure unweaves
the substance, of flesh.

Below in the
under house of rooms
only door spaces exist
& bulbs in bedding
   Boxed
endive in the dark, and then

the telephone, raucous, unfettered,
penetrates down
to a half light (this naked bulb)
out to the unfenced, unbounded
plot that slopes to the edge

Nightshift

Trays of black and steaming, the first chairs
pushed back, brigflats, snave, holywell -
leave be given to bring in a bill
for the quieting the subject, as diners mingle

the owlers met at buttdarts, midley and shorne
trampled on fleabane and squinancywort, tonight
the late hour in the hatch jumps with hip hop
and the jibe of the reggae man, as Betty and Bev

perch with ciggy and stem, and field
questions - what to do about the skins?
shove them out the back under the grain
against all pretences of concealment

let them rest from their haste, here may I
shove ha'pennies, down a mug or two
and drunkenly embrace, the closeness
that Jasmine left, and so I may rest

Salvaged

He sows salt on the gangway,
shoulders his burden, retraces
the steps to this sea-hidden
wordless song that lashes us,
indivisible, apart, voices that tell
cases to catch the spirits as they left
the depths we bear, so each
bottle filled by tide enters the porch
with a sense of liberation but
master, what changes these waves bring?

Listen, listen again at the edge of this lip
a blast of song, an infinite uproar
over shivers of ocean, where giant horses
bound into the sea among swimmers,

enrich, return to the world this beauty
for the enchantment of the moon
calms storms - genius
you all forge furrows with individual wakes.

Beyond the stone

This precious stone set in the silver sea
and a hubbub of players at sunrise
stumbling down, leather upon mud,
mud on stone, the sullen passage

of weary steps, faces sunswept,
rain tumbling through grey, along
this southern limb of the fold
beneath which the killas buckling,

slice upon slice, reveal flood creatures
that water patterns rustled light-years ago,
a heap of jewels lodged within, as bustling
folk shortly fill the reasonable shores.